BY THOMAS K. ADAMSON

THE HOUSTON
TEXANS
STORY

BELLWETHER MEDIA · MINNEAPOLIS, MN

Are you ready to take it to the extreme? Torque books thrust you into the action-packed world of sports, vehicles, mystery, and adventure. These books may include dirt, smoke, fire, and chilling tales. **WARNING**: read at your own risk.

This edition first published in 2017 by Bellwether Media, Inc.

No part of this publication may be reproduced in whole or in part without written permission of the publisher. For information regarding permission, write to Bellwether Media, Inc., Attention: Permissions Department, 5357 Penn Avenue South, Minneapolis, MN 55419.

Library of Congress Cataloging-in-Publication Data

Names: Adamson, Thomas K., 1970-
Title: The Houston Texans Story / by Thomas K. Adamson.
Description: Minneapolis, MN : Bellwether Media, Inc., 2017. | Series:
   Torque: NFL Teams | Includes bibliographical references and index. |
   Audience: Ages: 7-12. | Audience: Grades: 3 through 7.
Identifiers: LCCN 2016002572 | ISBN 9781626173675 (hardcover : alk. paper)
Subjects: LCSH: Houston Texans (Football team)–History–Juvenile literature.
Classification: LCC GV956.H69 A33 2017 | DDC 796.332/64097641411
LC record available at http://lccn.loc.gov/2016002572

Printed in the United States of America, North Mankato, MN.

TABLE OF CONTENTS

The date is January 7, 2012. The Houston Texans face the Cincinnati Bengals in their first-ever **playoff** game. There is less than a minute left in the first half. The game is tied at 10.

J.J.
Watt

Defensive end J.J. Watt leaps to **intercept** a pass. He runs the ball into the end zone. Touchdown! The cheers of 71,725 fans fill the stadium.

T.J.
Yates

Late in the third quarter, **quarterback**
T.J. Yates throws a long pass. **Wide receiver**
Andre Johnson is open. He makes the catch.
Another touchdown! The Texans now lead 24
to 10. They win their first playoff game with a
final score of 31 to 10.

Andre Johnson

SCORING TERMS

END ZONE

the area at each end of a football field; a team scores by entering the opponent's end zone with the football.

EXTRA POINT

a score that occurs when a kicker kicks the ball between the opponent's goal posts after a touchdown is scored; 1 point.

FIELD GOAL

a score that occurs when a kicker kicks the ball between the opponent's goal posts; 3 points.

SAFETY

a score that occurs when a player on offense is tackled behind his own goal line; 2 points for defense.

TOUCHDOWN

a score that occurs when a team crosses into its opponent's end zone with the football; 6 points.

TWO-POINT CONVERSION

a score that occurs when a team crosses into its opponent's end zone with the football after scoring a touchdown; 2 points.

The Texans are the newest team in the National Football League (NFL). They began playing in 2002.

Houston made it to the playoffs three times between the years 2012 and 2016. They quickly became known for their tough **defense**.

Home games are played at NRG Stadium in Houston, Texas. It was the first NFL stadium with a **retractable** roof. The roof only takes 7 minutes to open and close.

It is made of metal and cloth. Natural light pours in through the fabric.

HOUSTON,
TEXAS

The Texans play in the South **Division** of the American Football **Conference** (AFC). The Tennessee Titans are their main division **rival**.

But Houston has another rival closer to home. The Texans love chances to battle the Dallas Cowboys. In their first game ever, the Texans beat the Cowboys 19 to 10!

NFL DIVISIONS

 AFC

AFC NORTH

 BALTIMORE **RAVENS**

 CINCINNATI **BENGALS**

 CLEVELAND **BROWNS**

 PITTSBURGH **STEELERS**

AFC EAST

 BUFFALO **BILLS**

 MIAMI **DOLPHINS**

 PATRIOTS

 NEW YORK **JETS**

AFC SOUTH

 TEXANS

 INDIANAPOLIS **COLTS**

 JACKSONVILLE **JAGUARS**

 TENNESSEE **TITANS**

AFC WEST

 DENVER **BRONCOS**

 CHIEFS

 OAKLAND **RAIDERS**

 SAN DIEGO **CHARGERS**

NFC

NFC NORTH

 CHICAGO **BEARS**

 DETROIT **LIONS**

GREEN BAY **PACKERS**

MINNESOTA **VIKINGS**

NFC EAST

DALLAS **COWBOYS**

GIANTS

 PHILADELPHIA **EAGLES**

 WASHINGTON **REDSKINS**

NFC SOUTH

 FALCONS

 CAROLINA **PANTHERS**

NEW ORLEANS **SAINTS**

 BUCCANEERS

NFC WEST

 CARDINALS

 LOS ANGELES **RAMS**

 SAN FRANCISCO **49ERS**

 SEATTLE **SEAHAWKS**

13

Football fans in Texas cheered for the Houston Oilers from 1960 to 1996. But the Oilers moved to Tennessee in 1997. Their name changed to the Titans two years later. Fans in Houston wanted an NFL team back.

Houston Oilers, 1978 season

2002 season

The NFL finally awarded an **expansion team** to Houston in 1999. The Texans hit the field in 2002.

The Houston Texans have had some great seasons. Others have not been so great. Their best season was 2012. They had a **winning record** of 12-4.

The next year, they stunned fans by losing 14 games in a row. Nonetheless, the Texans won AFC South Division titles in 2011, 2012, and 2015.

TIMELINE

1999

Awarded to Houston as an NFL expansion team

2002

Played first regular season game, beating the Dallas Cowboys (19-10)

2009

Signed running back Arian Foster

2000

Named the Houston Texans

2003

Drafted wide receiver Andre Johnson

2009

Had first-ever winning season with 9 wins and 7 losses

2013

Won first playoff game of the 2012 season, beating the Cincinnati Bengals

19 FINAL SCORE **13**

2011

Drafted defensive end J.J. Watt

2015

Earned the AFC South Division title for the third time in five seasons

2012

Won first-ever playoff game, beating the Cincinnati Bengals

31 FINAL SCORE **10**

2016

Celebrated J.J. Watt being named NFL Defensive Player of the Year for the third time

Houston has had some standout players. Andre Johnson was the first in the NFL to make at least 60 catches in each of his first eight seasons.

In 2010, **running back** Arian Foster led the NFL in **rushing yards**. Tackle Duane Brown is a fierce protector for Houston's quarterbacks.

Andre Johnson

Duane Brown

A TEXAN MVP

Matt Schaub was named Most Valuable Player (MVP) in the 2010 Pro Bowl. He completed 13 of 17 passes that game.

No Texan has been a better leader on defense than J.J. Watt. He won Defensive Player of the Year for the 2012, 2014, and 2015 seasons.

Brian Cushing also helps the team's defense. He adds strength and speed.

TEAM GREATS

ANDRE JOHNSON
WIDE RECEIVER
2003-2014

MATT SCHAUB
QUARTERBACK
2007-2013

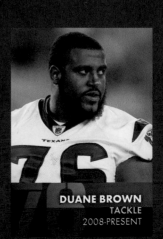

DUANE BROWN
TACKLE
2008-PRESENT

GETTING THE QUARTERBACK

Watt was the first player in NFL history to have more than 20 sacks in two different seasons.

ARIAN FOSTER
RUNNING BACK
2009-2015

BRIAN CUSHING
LINEBACKER
2009-PRESENT

J.J. WATT
DEFENSIVE END
2011-PRESENT

Texans fans rally behind their team. NRG Stadium has a special section for the wildest Texans fans. This area is called the Bull Pen. The rowdy crowd cheers, chants, and carries out game day traditions. The Texans Bull Pen Pep Band plays alongside them.

FULL OF MUSIC AND PEP

The Bull Pen Pep Band performs during time-outs and quarter breaks. They even play in the parking lot before games.

There is one game day tradition specific to the Texans. During player introductions, the crowd shows excitement for each player.

Brian Cushing

The announcer calls out a player's first name. The crowd then yells his last name. The Texans give fans plenty of reasons to make noise!

MORE ABOUT THE
TEXANS

Team name:
Houston Texans

Team name explained:
Named after the people
of Texas who are proud,
hardworking, and
independent

Joined NFL: 2002

Conference: **AFC**

Division: **South**

Main rivals: **Tennessee Titans,
Dallas Cowboys**

Hometown: **Houston, Texas**

Training camp location: **Houston Methodist Training Center, Houston, Texas**

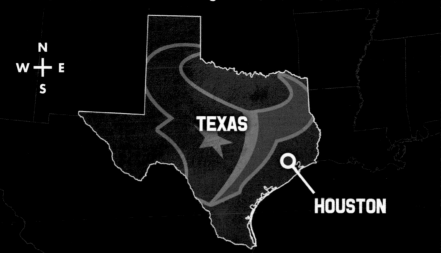

N
W—E
S

TEXAS

HOUSTON

Home stadium name: **NRG Stadium**

Stadium opened: **2002**

Seats in stadium: **72,220**

Logo: **The head of a bull with a five-pointed star that represents Texas and its people**

Colors: **Blue, red, white**

Mascot: **Toro**

GLOSSARY

conference—a large grouping of sports teams that often play one another

defense—the group of players who try to stop the opposing team from scoring

defensive end—a player on defense whose job is to tackle the player with the ball

division—a small grouping of sports teams that often play one another; usually there are several divisions of teams in a conference.

expansion team—a new team added to a sports league

intercept—to catch a pass thrown by the opposing team

playoff—a game played after the regular NFL season is over; playoff games determine which teams play in the Super Bowl.

quarterback—a player on offense whose main job is to throw and hand off the ball

retractable—able to open and close

rival—a long-standing opponent

running back—a player on offense whose main job is to run with the ball

rushing yards—yards gained by running with the ball

wide receiver—a player on offense whose main job is to catch passes from the quarterback

winning record—when a team has more wins than losses in a season

TO LEARN MORE

AT THE LIBRARY

Frisch, Nate. *Story of the Houston Texans*. Mankato, Minn.: Creative Education, 2014.

Stewart, Mark. *The Houston Texans*. Chicago, Ill.: Norwood House Press, 2013.

Wyner, Zach. *Houston Texans*. New York, N.Y.: AV2 by Weigl, 2015.

ON THE WEB

Learning more about the Houston Texans is as easy as 1, 2, 3.

1. Go to www.factsurfer.com.

2. Enter "Houston Texans" into the search box.

3. Click the "Surf" button and you will see a list of related web sites.

With factsurfer.com, finding more information is just a click away.

INDEX